Learn how to order your favorite dim sum dishes!

Written Format

English Translation

Simplified Chinese Characters

Yale Romanization + Tone Numbers

Complimentary audio reading available at steaminghappiness.com

What kind of tea would you like?

饮咩茶?

yam² me¹ cha⁴

Jasmine
香片
heung¹ pin²

Shou Mei
寿眉
sau⁶ mei⁴

Pu'er

普洱

pou² nei²

Chrysanthemum

菊花

guk¹ fa¹

A Blend of Pu-Er and Chrysanthemum

菊普

guk¹ pou²

Dragon Well

龙井

lung^4 jeng^2

Oolong

乌龙

wu^1 lung^2

Eat Dim Sum

食点心
sik⁶ dim² sam¹

Pork and Shrimp Dumpling

烧卖

siu¹ maai⁶

Glutinous Rice Dumpling

咸水角

haam⁴ seui² gok²

Shrimp Dumpling

虾饺
ha¹ gaau²

Beef Ball

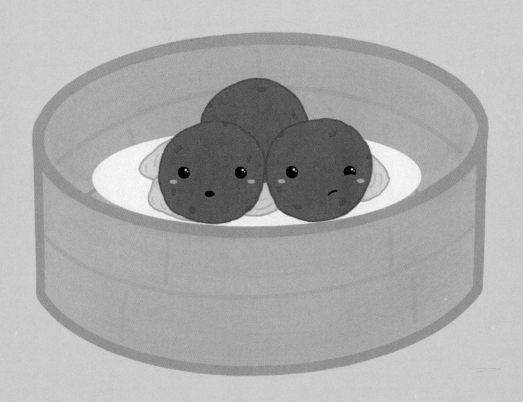

牛肉丸

ngau⁴ yuk⁶ yun⁴

Pan-fried Pork Bun

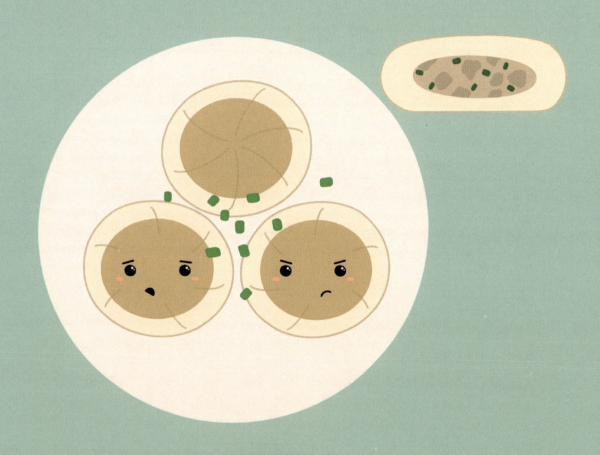

生煎包

saang¹ jin¹ baau¹

Braised Chicken Feet

凤爪

fung⁶ jaau²

Shrimp Rice Noodle Roll

虾肠

ha¹ cheung⁴

Chinese Donut Rice Noodle Roll

炸两

ja³ leung²

Rice Noodle Roll

肠粉

cheung² fan²

Bean Curd Roll

鲜竹卷

sin¹ juk¹ gyun²

Radish Cake

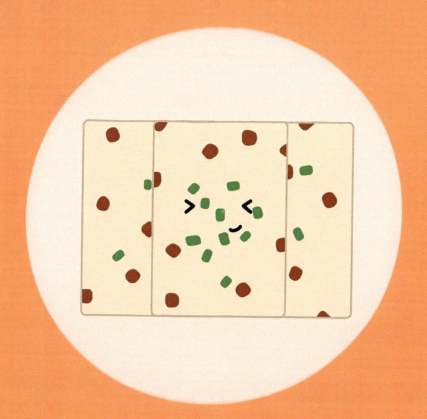

萝卜糕

lo⁴ baak⁶ gou¹

Sticky Rice with Chicken
(Wrapped in Lotus Leaf)

糯米鸡

no^6 mai^5 gai^1

Malay Sponge Cake

马拉糕

ma⁵ laai¹ gou¹

BBQ Pork Bun

叉烧包

cha¹ siu¹ baau¹

Spareribs with Black Bean Sauce

排骨

paai⁴ gwat¹

Crispy Taro Puff

芋角

wu⁶ gok³

Sesame Ball

煎堆

jin¹ deui¹

Egg Custard Bun

奶黄包

naai⁵ wong⁴ baau¹

Century Egg and Pork Congee

皮蛋瘦肉粥

pei⁴ daan² sau³ yuk⁶ juk¹

Fish Fillet Congee

鱼片粥

yu⁴ pin² juk¹

Egg Tart

蛋挞

daan⁶ taat¹

This book is dedicated to my family, who gave up everything and moved across the world to a place of unfamiliarity to give my sister and I a better life. Words cannot express how eternally grateful I am for their sacrifices, unconditional love and support.

張 ♥ 余

Made in the USA
Middletown, DE
08 April 2021